THESE THOUGHTS ARE OURS

Edited by

Joanne Baxter

First published in Great Britain in 1999 by
POETRY NOW
Remus House,
Coltsfoot Drive,
Woodston,
Peterborough, PE2 9JX
Telephone (01733) 898101
Fax (01733) 313524

All Rights Reserved

Copyright Contributors 1999

HB ISBN 0 75430 737 9
SB ISBN 0 75430 738 7

FOREWORD

Although we are a nation of poets we are accused of not reading poetry, or buying poetry books. After many years of listening to the incessant gripes of poetry publishers, I can only assume that the books they publish, in general, are books that most people do not want to read.

Poetry should not be obscure, introverted, and as cryptic as a crossword puzzle: it is the poet's duty to reach out and embrace the world.

The world owes the poet nothing and we should not be expected to dig and delve into a rambling discourse searching for some inner meaning.

The reason we write poetry (and almost all of us do) is because we want to communicate: an ideal; an idea; or a specific feeling. Poetry is as essential in communication, as a letter; a radio; a telephone, and the main criteria for selecting the poems in this anthology is very simple: they communicate.

CONTENTS

My Heart	Helen Preston	1
It's Spring Again	D M Jackson	2
Coming Of Age?	T Eccleston	3
Two Young Men	Maureen Anne Browne	4
Delusions Of The Mind	Laurence Idell	6
Washing Day	Pat Melbourn	7
Memories	Isobel Dorward Blythe	8
Night Sounds	Anne Biggs	9
Evening	Leonard Jeffries	10
Night Whispers	Mary Green	13
Painful Night	Wendy Ray	14
Good Night?	Alfred J Smith	15
Night Demons	Josephine Duthie	16
Fear Of The Night	Linda Brown	17
Amber And Pearl	Audra Ann Murphy	18
By Oneself Perturbance	Hilary Jill Robson	19
Dark Pain	Dennis Packham	20
School Thoughts At Night	Dorothy Whitehall	21
A Little Night Musing	Maria-Christina	22
Night V Day	Frieda Cox	23
Half Light Illusions	Warren Galley	24
Come Back Home Dear	Leslie F Dukes	25
Night Whispers	Elizabeth Cowley-Guscott	26
Dark Deception	Ruth Daviat	27
Whispers Of The Night	Lee Rosa	28
Please Do Go Gentle Into Life's Good Night	Solomon Blue Waters	29
Whatever Next?	Denny Rhymer	30
Cyberworld . . .	Stephen Gyles	31
No Place For Me	S Mullinger	32
Today's Effects On The Future	Nigel Wilton Foster	33
A Terrible Place	Josephine Bottino	34
The Day Of The Comet	John Hill	35
Today's Effects On The Future	Dan Chellumben	36
Summer Holidays	Norma A MacArthur	37
Summer Holidays	Tamsin Burley	38

On A Beach In June	Kelly Hearns	39
Holiday Blues	Jeanne Walker	40
At The Water Hole	Kim Montia	41
Summer (?) Holiday	Anne Byron	42
Up Here When I Fly	Jennifer Abdulazeez	43
Poetic Dream	Mary Skelton	44
Destinations	Julia Cutting	45
Summer Holiday	Kellyann Cochrane	46
Tomorrow And Tomorrow And Tomorrow	Tilla B Smith	47
Holiday Mystique	Renée Duckworth	48
The Storm Petrel	G E Khandelwal	49
The Illustrious Scot (An Ode To Alex Ferguson)	Ian Barton	50
Ringing Up The Changes	Jon El Wright & Jackdaw	51
Just Remember	T G Bloodworth	52
Boys	Kirsty Towle	53
Black Valley	Ann Beard	54
Austria	Ben Forbes	56
Africa	Alexander Foot	57
Canada	Adam Carter	58
New York	Kayleigh Bromell	60
To Darren	Esther Hawkins	61
Lytham	Teresa Booth	62
My Holiday	Sandra Rose	63
Summer Holidays	Just Tom Sexton	64
Shhhh . . .	Angel Robinson	65
In My Mind's Eye	Jo Howson	66
Brighton By The Sea	Alexandra Ayton	67
Unnecessary	Elsa D Wilson	68
The Big Apple	M Saqib Hussain	69
Summer Holiday	Ghazanfer Eqbal	70
Looking Forward	Catherine Whittaker	71
This Summer	Naomi Elisa Price	72
Holidays	Barbara E Stubbs	73
Holiday Moods	Brenda Holland	74
Summer Holiday - Then And Now	Corinne Lovell	75

Summer Holiday	Sylvia M Harbert	76
The Way They Were	Rose Marie Morris	77
Arcadia Baltic Cruise	Alice M Archer	78
Never Alone	G Read	79
Perfect Bliss	Amy Webb	80
Mud Eater	Mary G Kane	81
Somewhere In Andalucia	Ian Fyles	82
In The Arms Of The Moon	Christine Denise Wells	83
Maiden Voyage	Ann Hathaway	84
Summer Holiday	Jenny Youngs	85
Summer Holidays	Rebecca Heard	86
The Beach	Sophie Walter	87
Summer	Karla Webb	88
Australia	Ashley Withey	89
Africa	Muna Ngenda	90
Italia	Ryan Kewley	91
Australia	Sarah Heard	92
Florida Sun	Katie Furniss	93
Eastbourne	Margaret Andrews	94
Move Over - Noah	Beryl Mapperley	96
The Spanish Senorita	Glenys M Bowell	97
At Home In Holidayland	Helga I Dharmpaul	98
Lac St. Bonnet, Troncais	Kathy Butler	99
Holiday Hell	M Ekins	100
Fistral Bay	Roy Hedgcock	101
Seaside Holiday!	Margaret McHugh	102
Go To Croatia	Kristina Kastelan	103

My Heart

My heart is full of love, and warmth, and also overwhelmed.
It's tender, and it's loving, it keeps me going on,
but at times you feel that life is hard, you have to carry on.
But sometimes, when you're in despair, there's hope somewhere.
In desperate need, you look for love, you feel there is a need,
love is deep, within the heart, makes you warm,
but will not part. Although your mind is all mixed up,
and does not know which way to turn, love will help you on your way.
It could be right, it could be wrong, when you are in despair.
Although you feel so cold and weak and helpless in every way,
the warmth of love, will keep you warm, and help you to survive.
I look at life, in many ways and realise my hopes and fears
but there are people worse than me and realise they're in need,
so when life's tough, and very hard, don't give up,
there's hope you see, because I've been in desperate need.
Just think of love it helps you strive, and you will see it through,
without the love, you can't get by, and this is how I feel.

Helen Preston

IT'S SPRING AGAIN

Winter is over
Spring has arrived
The buds on the trees
Are given new life

The daffodils are in bloom
So are the crocuses
You can sit down and stare
As life makes new progress

The weather improves
It gets warmer each day
The daylight lasts longer
Summer is on its way.

Winter is over
And spring is here
Let's hope it's a good one
As it begins a new year

D M Jackson

COMING OF AGE?

Has winter arrived so soon? Years are massing.
It seems time is in such a darned big hurry,
And I ache because of its passing.
Summer was only yesterday.

How the years are crowding in relentlessly,
And memories fade of long past joys.
Old age creeps up silently
Then shouts too loudly, 'I'm here, I'm here!'

What happened to my goals?
Did I ever achieve anything at all?
Oh, what a waste, a shameful waste, such a waste of time,
And life is so much nearer to its final call.

Curse these old bones and aching muscles,
For time to laze I haven't got.
I have far too much to accomplish
In my last few years. But what? But what?

T Eccleston

Two Young Men

One, a soldier - a patriot too;
Whatever his country asked he'd do.
His country asked: set a people free;
Stem the tide of a communist sea.

With high ideals the young man went;
Fighting for justice was the intent.
'Twas a sense of right that spurred him so;
He made his choice, and he chose to go.

The other, a college lad, was *sent*:
He wasn't a soldier, but he went
To defend his country from attack:
The intruder just kept coming back.

But he fought bravely, and he fought well,
And saw for himself, that war is hell.
Now he had a diff'rent point of view,
But he would fight for his country too.

Each fought hard and with equal intent,
And neither side inclined to relent.
A war of attrition was raging
With young men dying, young men ageing.

War played on the nerves, played on the mind,
Reason and sense were harder to find.
Frustration, fear, distorted the view;
Paradise burned; its people did too.

Three decades on the questions remain:
How did it happen? What did we gain?
So much destruction, so much was lost,
Nations involved still counting the cost.

And the soldier? He didn't survive,
Yet the other one came out alive,
And he thought he'd won, but knew he'd lost
When he looked around and saw the cost.

We'll not be so quick to ask again
The lives of more than a million men
In order to change a point of view;
Values *you* hold, don't always hold true.

Maureen Anne Browne

DELUSIONS OF THE MIND

Fast flows the growing stimuli
of inner thought, as dragons
convey the freedom of immortal
souls, showering their fiery
discord on the fleeting transience
of ingrained beliefs.
Rejoicing in the enlightenment
that permeates the explication
of our unfulfilled desires,
only taking succour from
the delusions that transfix
those aspirations protected by
impermeable cortices.

Laurence Idell

WASHING DAY

Washing day - I liked it best!
I think it was the smell
Of the cleanest washing in the land -
O everyone could tell!

Washed with 'Lux' the toilet soap
And hung out in the breeze.
Folk would laugh at my delight -
They always loved to tease.

The dolly pegs were numerous -
I handled them with care
To peg some Long Johns on the line
Absorbing nice fresh air.

The towels, the socks and all 'the smalls'
Danced for hours and hours.
I only brought them back inside
When the sunlight turned to showers.

Washing day I liked it best.
When all is said and done -
There's nothing like clean underwear
Dried by the wind and sun.

Pat Melbourn

MEMORIES

No more I'll see your happy smile, telephone and chat awhile
this sad, sad thing I had to do was call and say goodbye to you.
I kissed your thin and weary face, full of courage, full of grace,
took your hand and said 'Love you', you whispered back
                                                'Love you too'.
I've never had to say 'Goodbye' to a loved one about to die.
Now that Christmas is drawing near, I remember us in childhood dear
as we raced each other down the stair to see if Santa had been there.
In summer I visit our secret place, every footstep to retrace
our secret island, o the fun where we played until the setting sun.
Through the trees came a shining ray, I felt your presence all the day.
O sister how the years can race, I'm closer to you in this place,
where in summer days we loved to roam, instead of by
                                        your cold gravestone.
They say there's sunshine after rain, some day soon I'll cope again,
there's been many grey days in my life full of heartache, full of strife.
It seems my heart will just not mend, I miss you so dear sister friend.
From childhood to middle years we never dreamed there would be tears
now I sit here all alone, another sister has gone home.

Isobel Dorward Blythe

Night Sounds

The growing darkness
    Clears my mind,
The soft dark shadows
    Look blended and kind,
Rustles in hedges,
    Owls up in trees,
With time for reflection,
    Not busy like bees,
The step of a stray cat,
    The screech of a black bat,
The day's beating drum,
    Night's quiet hum,
The only sound heard,
    Is not of a bird,
But the sound on the grass,
    Of my feet as they pass.

Anne Biggs

EVENING

The vale of Ogmore nestles low
beneath five proud imposing hills
and down the middle of the vale
a river runs o'er rocks and stones
and out into the cultured world,
watched by the half-soaked half-veiled eyes
of small stone streets that line the way
or climb the slopes on either side . . .
and coming in from out the world
as if to see what lies within,
the road and railway nose their ways
like bloodhounds to the hindmost hill.

'Tis evening here, the chattery day
is stifled as the hand of dusk
is pressed upon these darkening hills:
Small boys are hauled in off the streets
and lines of washing from the backs:
The chimneys lose their languorous haze
and suddenly puff into life,
and night slides down like rubble slides
down slag-heaps on the hills.

The night is young. The cooling skies
watch with a million starry eyes
the mountains squat around the vale
like Indian squaws around a fire:
the streets grow hollow as the houses
sulk behind the narrow backs
of tall street lights with bended necks
that stare so bare-faced either way
the shadows stand afraid to pass
unless behind the passers-by.

Beware this hour, this magic hour
when night must stretch 'fore settling down:
when all the secrets of the soul
receive their sustenance!
Now Yanto sits beside his pint
and thinks he's much the luckier man
than Owen sat home with his wife
and David courting with his girl,
who think they're much the luckier men
than Idris who has got no girl,
no house, no wife, no pint of beer,
but lodges up at Yanto's house,
where now he sits on Yanto's couch
by Yanto's fire, with Yanto's wife,
wond'ring how long his luck will last
whilst eating Yanto's supper.

This magic hour when through the windows
of the little rooms upstairs
the cold night peers and tries to frighten
little children just in bed!
This magic hour when lovers make
soft speeches with their trembling lips
and hearts melt in the fragrance of
Shakespearean eloquence.
Oh God, to think that at this hour
young Bessie Jones from up the street
is out with Dai, the butcher's boy,
and she a married woman!
And John the Preacher steals a kiss from
Maggie Dripping, second-house!
How many broken hearts and vows
for she's a married woman?

And in the Book, for he who turned
against the Lord the cock crowed thrice.
How many cocks, in retrospect,
will crow and crow and crow tonight?

Leonard Jeffries

NIGHT WHISPERS

Night whispers, what do I hear?
   Peace and quiet, and tranquillity,
I'm huddled away in my cosy bed
   There is nothing to dread.

I'm away from that infernal news
   Who's dead, or who shot who?
From ethnic cleansing, weeping and wailing
   Not knowing what to do.

Lights out, where have I gone?
   Most of the night to slumberland
I hear the dawn chorus.
   And the clock striking seven
Or did I dream, it was heaven?

Mary Green

PAINFUL NIGHT

As we enter the hospital
by the emergency door,
fear and worry follow us
for we don't know the score.

My husband's eyes are playing up,
in fact, he's lost his sight,
will they find out what is wrong,
will they put it right?

Night life in the hospital
is as busy as the day,
nurses rush, the phones ring out,
and doctors make their way

to help the poor unfortunates
for whom the sirens wail,
those for whom life's been cut short
and those like us who fail

to be ill during daylight hours.
Deep in the night they let me stay
and sit amidst their bustle
till 2am I'm on my way.

As I step into the cool night air,
away from people's hurt and pain,
two nightingales in nearby trees
sing out their clear and pure refrain.

Despite the troubles that we meet
those night birds showed me life is sweet.

Wendy Ray

GOOD NIGHT?

When night at last slips bonds of day and, sun sinks out of vision,
You might just hear the darkness say, in tones of clear precision,
'I have the moon, I have the stars, I have the Milky Way,
Begone until tomorrow morn, for you have had your day.'

But night's a subtle fellow, with a thousand different faces,
Perceived in countless different ways, in countless different places.
A blessing to the tired and weary; dreamless sleep for many,
A pause between backbreaking days, where hope there's barely any.

A touch, as light as angel's kiss, a cloak of gentle down,
Protecting those who see it thus, portraying nature's gown.
And in this garb night's recognised, as beneficent donor,
By countless hordes within its thrall, to worship, love and honour.

But night can be a surly brute, as in the wings he waits,
For centre stage his one desire, his pre-determined fate.
He lowers, glowers and terrifies, the innocent and meek,
And villains love his black embrace, as they their havoc wreak.

Night is an enigma then; to some; black-hearted fellow.
But others love his peaceful mien and find him gently mellow.
When tranquil disposition reigns, the sky portrays sheer magic.
At other times his masking cloak, has consequences tragic.

Is night true independent then? With purpose, course to run?
Or has it just supporting role, beneath a setting sun?
Some say it's day in evening dress, with stars its flashing jewels,
And lunar light mellifluous, shows heaven's limpid pools.

But justice demands equity and, truth should always out,
With true conclusions fairly reached, removing cant and doubt.
The night is a necessity, presents a breathing space,
In separating day from day, a boon to human race.

Alfred J Smith

NIGHT DEMONS

I lie curled
in maternal warmth
floating on an island of sanctuary.
A sea of invisible grotesques
flood my imagination
and distort the shadows of darkness.
I slide deeper
into the wombed mantel
hiding from self-made demons.
They haunt my mind
and stab each nerve
with pinpricks of alarm.
Images of fear
seep through my cocoon.
I am threatened
with an irresistible urge
to reveal my presence
as the night creates its monsters.
Each movement
throws noise at my senses.
Sharp echoes bleed adrenaline into the air,
- I tense, waiting.
Minutes melt my stronghold of comfort.
A heavy weight drags,
my breath quickens,
I clutch at my quilted shield.
The night demon whispers
hot air across my cheek - I am lost.
- 'Good night sweetheart.'

Josephine Duthie

FEAR OF THE NIGHT

Waiting ages for a taxicab but still not one in sight
I don't think I better loiter so late on Friday night
It's time for the pubs to close, many drunken youths about
Down town the sound of fighting is starting to break out

If only I hadn't missed the last bus, I wouldn't be here alone
As I decide to be brave and chance the long lonely walk home
The sound of distant footsteps makes my blood start to creep
Oh how I wish I was at home in bed, safely fast asleep

My pace of walk is getting quicker, almost a gentle run
Being approached by strangers late at night, isn't any fun
Maybe it's just harmless, but horror fills my head
I cry out, let me be, as I fearfully run in dread

I head off in another direction, this gang I want to lose
I don't want to be the headlines, the paper's horrific news
The sound of laughter echoes as they run off down a side street
Leaving just an eerie stillness and the sound of my own feet

I start to feel much safer once I turn into the lane
The fear starts to leave me and my composure I regain
Tonight my path is dimly lit, just the odd street light
Low clouds fill the sky and no stars are shining bright

The scurrying of a rabbit, the hoot of a barn owl
The mournful cry of the ginger tom-cat whilst out on the prowl
Strange sounds break the silence, from the creatures of the night
The time for them to come to life, now it's not daylight

Delving into my pocket, to find my front door key
The sanctuary of my cottage, is now in front of me
The nightmare of my journey home, starts to fade away
Such things would never scare me, in the light of day.

Linda Brown

AMBER AND PEARL

How the dawn so gracefully lifts the peace
of a new fresh day that it brings,
with outside the window birds chirp and sing
as the wind lifts them catching under their wings.

And yet when dusk falls upon the sky is like fire
and another night unfolds,
curtains pulled to shut out that cry of
fighting cats, foxes and owls.

The city streets are busy and high
are voices and sirens which screech,
crowds gather and roads that are friendly and clear
that long secluded walk taken without even a thought of fear.

Yet that same busy city becomes a mass of bright lights
and unfamiliarity insight brings a chill,
volumes increased and that once friendly road
holds a danger and on your own wouldn't dare go.

Taking the dog along the sea front or cliffs
that field which is heavily overgrown,
greeting a stranger who is also taking in air
and start a conversation in the interest you share.

But once more the whispers that the evenings bring
enhances the dangers which inside us alarm rings,
forcing the evening walks to remain short
hurrying quickly never stand to talk.

Highlighten dangers on what we watch and read
perhaps makes the difference and so caution we heed,
as through the night we keep open an ear
sense of seeing is blind and our only option is to hear.

An explanation therefore I feel is natural instinct for our self survival
with the night bringing obscurity until the next mornings arrival.

Audra Ann Murphy

BY ONESELF PERTURBANCE

From security of comforting light
Step into a moonless night,
Own movements cause unnerving disturbance,
Stressing being by oneself perturbance.

Lightness into warmth of sunlight brightness
Shears fleece of coy sheepishness,
Emerge unnoticed, slip in and converge
Into city motion soundlessly submerge.

Darkness fans louts noxious bullying aims,
Kicks prejudice into flames,
Butts jaundiced eye views of cowardly gangs,
Provoking fights from undesired harangues.

Angling in peace of tranquil countryside,
Still, becalmed at riverside,
Or lolled against tree reading, picnicking,
Lulled by music of birds, cool water trickling.

The Moon casts shadows thro' tree canopy,
A gust rustles dead leaves free,
Trunks become lie-in-wait ambush places,
Burrs, knurs and holes turn into watching faces.

Imagination, wary listening ear
And solitude create fear,
Twig underfoot, prowling cat, light warning flare,
Night-time spins dream places into nightmares.

Hilary Jill Robson

DARK PAIN

I walk the dark streets
Still wet from the evening rain,
Dark streets, such dark streets,
But not as dark as the pain
That burns within my heart.

I walk the dark streets
And yet I walk in vain,
For this darkest of nights
Cannot hide this pain
That lives within my heart.

I walk the dark streets,
The darkness to conceal my plight,
When a shaft of light appears
As dawn breaks to end the night
But not the pain within my heart.

When oh when, I ask
Will my heart be as light
As the wakening dawn I see
Through tired and misty eyes,
While pain still burns within my heart.

For it's such pain I feel
As pictures flicker in my head
Like silent films, reel after reel,
As they will until I'm dead
And the pain is stilled within my heart.

Dennis Packham

SCHOOL THOUGHTS AT NIGHT

The clock strikes nine, one dark, stormy night,
How busy we have been all day:
The children and staff have all gone home,
And soon I'll be on my way.

I've switched off the lights, one by one,
I've closed all the windows and doors:
Is that the creaking of the ancient boards?
Or the missing hamster, scuttling across the floors?

I'm in the hall, the central point,
Wind and rain through the windows call:
I'm safe and secure in our old school,
Oh dear! Someone's work has fallen off the wall.

Hush - can I hear the lessons of the past?
When staff were oh so strict.
Not, Jean and Barbara and Catherine, Eva and Mona and Sue,
Tricia and Sandra, all by me hand-picked.

Is my imagination playing tricks?
Do I hear tables being chanted clearly?
Four times three and five times ten,
Voices sounding oh so weary.

My memory picks up a change of tune,
Sweet voices all singing together:
Then with a jerk, I come back to earth,
The only sound is that of the weather.

Well, now at last, I must go home,
Clutching the old key, ready to turn,
Tomorrow is another day,
Full of surprises and children, eager to learn.

Dorothy Whitehall

A Little Night Musing

'Now I lay me down to sleep,
I pray the Lord my soul to keep.
If I should die before I wake
I ask the Lord my soul to take.'

So we were taught as children -
But I would rather not
Die before I wake -
There's so much I want to do!

My heart is pounding away
And I wait for it to stop.
My lungs are still functioning
So I know I'm alive.

Perhaps I should stay awake
And wait, for 'Death doth know his hour'
And 'No moment is guaranteed' -
Perhaps I shouldn't go to sleep!

Suppose I do die tonight,
Who will feed the cats?
Would I be missed - who would
Find my body - and when?

The sun is shining -
It's Sunday morning.
I have experienced death
And resurrection - I thank God
For this new day.

Maria-Christina

NIGHT V DAY

The darkness closes round us like a mantle warm, but black
And fears become obsessions, we're afraid to turn our back.

Is it because we cannot see what lurks around each bend,
The unknown may be waiting as our nerves shake at their end.

Each shape becomes a monster and each sound a menace too
As in solitude and silence we sit there feeling blue.

The daylight changes everything for now we see quite clearly
That nothing's really lurking round, imagination merely.

The sounds we hear are normal now as every other day
And the silence of the darkness the light drives right away.

Our state of mind would alter if courage we should take
Let the light defeat the darkness for everybody's sake.

Find a place in the light where folk are mostly kind,
Face the sun and then the shadows will always fall behind.

Frieda Cox

HALF LIGHT ILLUSIONS

A dim sparsely lit street
Stretched out before me.
Boarded up shops
cars with only three wheels,
(not Reliants).
Kids from nine to nineteen
hanging around street corners,
drinking, smoking?
The dark hiding identities.

I continued walking
not drawing attention to myself;
then I was alone!
I must not run!
As I crossed a road I saw her.
Looking in a shop window.
But even with her back turned
she heard me and
walked away, quickly.
The dark hiding her identity.

I followed at a distance
slowly gaining with each step;
her heels click-clacking
on the broken pavement,
hips swaying, hair swaying,
shinning in the lamplight.
'Don't be afraid.' I called.
'Can I walk with you?' I asked.
She turned to look at me.
A bearded face stared at me
as a hairy fist struck.
My darkness hiding *his* identity.

Warren Galley

COME BACK HOME DEAR

He, or she is but a lonely child
They wander all alone,
Along the streets of 'Anywhere'
For they are the ones without a home
You can see them on the corners of any street in town
Most passing by they don't notice them -
And those that do . . . just frown;
    From the shadows a 'Pimp' is watching
Their where, and every move
Now comes the time to approach this child -
With the words . . . 'Can I help you Love?'
'Tis the first friendly word they've heard;
Now they're both in conversation
Soon he puts his hand upon their shoulder,
So friendly he seems to be,
'Come with me!' . . . I know a cafe, we'll have a cup of tea,
    The plot it's surely working, eating out of his hand,
The child's so young and naive . . . they don't understand;
A bed for the night with a roof above their head . . .
'Tis too much to refuse,
For their friends so nice, no thoughts have they
Their trust he will abuse,
Now their lives, they face ruin, by wandering from their home.
For those you meet along the street
Aren't always your friend,
For you left them, deciding you would roam -
But, if you had rung their number, of those you left behind
Then I'm sure you would have found,
A true friends voice, sure to answer -
'Come back home dear' . . . Please! come back home.

Leslie F Dukes

NIGHT WHISPERS

Septembers sun has set
It's reddish, darkness falls, I do not belong
Yet I know this street, when will morning come again?
My arm brushes ancient trees, rough bark
My feet trip over roots older than I, they do not talk
Today your leaves whispered to me
I smiled at your changing colours on my walk
Hurrying past the well of the drowned man
Where new houses stood, I pictured the old coal yard
Gone now like the entrance to the railway station
Why am I afraid and this return seem so hard?
The hump of the old bridge faces me
Climbing I peep over, below is a long empty track
Inside my head a train whistles, is that steam I see?
No, just a faint mist beginning to float towards a wreck
A lifeless building faces me shrouded in darkness
Once this was full of life, people laughed, machines roared
This is my ghost of yesterday, now a part of my restlessness
Scurrying past its emptiness, tears fell like morning dew
Soon to form on wild flowers in the hedge
No owl hooted, or fox crossed my path
Like as a child I hurried home to hide my face within my bed
What am I afraid of? I asked, slipping the key within its lock
Is it the night with many shadows
Or my mind's pictures showing creeping memories
Thoughts forgotten of youth and longings, summer's meadows
Entering a house of silence also dark
I told my thudding heart, tomorrow's near
Blackbird will sing, bees buzz, fears go, come see the park.

Elizabeth Cowley-Guscott

DARK DECEPTION

My old and weary feet traverse
empurpled thoroughfares;
I long to once again immerse
my soul, devoid of cares,
in music I have left behind,
its vibrant strains still light
in shadowed corners of my mind
whilst I confront the night.
Adventuring through symphony,
I hear each note anew
that thrilled me with expectancy
delightful evening through;
but now 'tis time to hit the road,
yet cloaked with beauteous sound;
Shall unseen dark device erode,
taint heaven that I found?
Now discord is dulling my brain;
an occasional gloom,
a hidden note I hear again -
does danger fiercely loom?
Genius of composer mad
splinters an evening's calm,
the night grows restless, moody, sad
and music loses its charm.
My solitude is insecure
and I look to stars for light,
yet further paradise to cure
the uncertainties of night.

Ruth Daviat

WHISPERS OF THE NIGHT

To lie awake in darkness, and the shadows of the night
Can colour our emotions - tone our senses black or white
Worries can invade our thoughts, they seem to multiply
Mentally revolving as the lonely hours go by
For some it can be frightening, anxiety sets in,
Others use it sleathily, to cover up their sins.
But darkness can bring sweet repose with stillness all around
It soothes the soul with silence and serenity is found
Is darkness lack of knowledge? Perhaps one day we'll find
The answer, while revealing the mysteries of the mind.
So long as there is darkness, there's no doubting we'll have light
And dawn will always come to end the whispers of the night.

Lee Rosa

PLEASE DO GO GENTLE INTO LIFE'S GOOD NIGHT
(with apologies to Dylan Thomas)

Please do go gentle into life's good night,
one wise of heart knows darkness sets light free;
fear not the sheer shadows of unknown sight.

Great change, my mother, she knows what is right,
alone bathes deepest wounds, soft sings to me:
Please do go gentle into life's good night.

Yet though the breaking of this shell I fight
with tiger tears so fierce I cannot see,
fear not the sheer shadows of unknown sight.

Too many tears were shed in days of bright,
this sunset of my soul I'll now agree;
please do go gentle into life's good night.

Ah! What a journey - filled with joys, such blight -
I've led to discover, for hard-won fee,
fear not the sheer shadows of unknown sight.

And at this pinnacle of lonely fright,
I hear my waiting mother's loving plea:
Please do go gentle into life's good night.
Fear not the sheer shadows of unknown sight.

Solomon Blue Waters

WHATEVER NEXT?

The robot will be programmed to smile,
More shopping will be door to door.
There'll be more demand for the computer,
And your robot will wash the floor!
Hopefully we'll all be greener -
Taking a leaf from the past:
War on want will be war on waste -
Making our possessions last!
There'll be more desire to have our say:
Spoken or written views;
But even with cable and satellite:
It will still be 'No news is good news!'
Personal transport will be the rocket;
Don't worry - the test drive will be to *Mars*.
When qualified, destination: *The Moon*,
And the scenery will be the stars!

Denny Rhymer

CYBERWORLD...

In the future
we may not be allowed
to talk
forbidden to think
speak
and gather wisdom
or exchange ideas
from living minds
to living minds . . .

Cybernetic machines
humming gadgets
jabbering alien squeaks
would transmit
their order direct to us
and their electronic pulses
would rob us of humanity
and transform us into
brain-drained slaves.

We must fight against
the electronic wizards
who programme the cybermachines
in a plan to conquer Earth
and initiate a ruthless dictatorship
of artificial intelligences.

Before mind-lost mankind would sink
into the cold abyss
of a sterile inhuman life
while compassion, love and understanding
from caring humankind
would be totally destroyed . . .

Stephen Gyles

No Place For Me

I've never been technologically minded,
Have no concept of working computers at all,
What an idea! Clones of myself all over the place.

I'm of the past, not the future, I've decided,
Can't contemplate televisions set into walls,
While lots of me seems a bad idea, very misplaced.

Can't play a video without being reminded,
That I must use some remote buttons, but not all,
So several just like me would be a disgrace.

S Mullinger

TODAY'S EFFECTS ON THE FUTURE

If I took a look into the future, year 2099,
I would only be guessing, because I'm twenty-nine.
The human race might exist,
If our spirits were like mist.
Something I'm sure we could not ignore,
Knocking on Heaven's door.
Scientist, technology, knowledge so free,
I bet they're not thinking, of the majority.
Only the money, and all the possibilities,
Of controlling man's destiny.

The minority controls the majority,
Who could destroy us genetically.
The joys of pregnancy, naturally,
Could be wiped out, with technology.
If we wanted test-tube babies,
To compete with technology,
What a phantom pregnancy.
I hope we all don't see, ourselves identically,
What a surprise it would be, living a life of misery,
In the year 2099 what a possibility.

Only one God can see,
Not man, and his technology
Nor all the government powers to be,
That could set our Mother Earth free,
If we all, had some dignity,
On today's effects of the future,
We cannot see, its up to you, and up to me
To set a standard, for our children to see.

Nigel Wilton Foster

A TERRIBLE PLACE

Where is this terrible place?
I don't know it anymore,
It's not the way it all began,
It no longer fits the plan.
Little children raped, abused, murdered in sheer terror,
Wrapped up in a bin bag by father, mother, brother,
All too horrendous to absorb - makes you want to shudder.

Where is this terrible place?
It's unbeknown to me,
It's heading for destruction,
For all eternity.
The hate, the greed, the wickedness,
The chaos and the murders,
Some sweet old grannies for a mere few pennies,
Mugged by some evil drug-filled thug - then murdered.

Where is this terrible place?
Filled with drugs, riots, violence,
Stress, strife and viciousness,
Why has mankind gone so far
In making this world such a mess?

Earthquakes, Bloodshed, Famines, Fires, Floods,
In the Bible was foretold,
In abundance in the very last days, unless mankind mend his ways.
Why can't man return to sanity before it is too late?
Make the world a wonderful place,
Spread love, kindness, respect for fellow man
Before he blows himself into space!

Josephine Bottino

THE DAY OF THE COMET

With reluctant sigh,
With thunderous pity,
With fiery anger and mournful eyes
For thoughtless cities and darkened minds,
Golden drop, heart deathly cold,
Shall fall from God Almighty.

This icy tear must fall to Earth,
The cynic's view but so too mine,
The selfish race -
The poison vine that grows in curve,
Must come to burn.

But from these ashes
Let dawn's light bring
A silence wide and dovelike wing
To span four corners for souls unselfish
As selfish as those once living -

To save God's beauty -
The gift of wisdom
That once had shone from children's eyes;
To claim with reason eternity's reach
From now, forever, and glittering prize.

John Hill

TODAY'S EFFECTS ON THE FUTURE

In a world of scientific invention
Where are carried on tests of genetic diseases
With new breakthroughs in treating cancer and aids
The world's leading intellects are preoccupied

As mankind moves toward the 21st century
Many wonder how the future will be like
Evidence is it will be a reflection of the past
Despite material progress in some places

Rampant is poverty, oppression, war and violence
One calamity after another the world has experienced
As a result of unsatisfactory human rule
Even today on a more damaging scale

In the early 1900's people were too civilised
That war was no longer possible, it was believed
Suddenly World War 1 brought the worst man-made catastrophe
At the end of this century
Continues man's domination over man to his injury
As being proved the sickening event in the Balkans.

Will the 21st century bring a better future?
Because of advances in industry, science and education
Scientific experiments on modified foods, test-tube babies, cloning
Do not, though, signal mankind's perfection
Rather a cause for concern
As already predicted in the Bible
Today's moral crisis would rock the world
Partly responsible is scientific progress
For the chemicals that have contributed
To the pollution of air, land, water and food.

Dan Chellumben

Summer Holidays

Where to go and what to do
Seems that I've been missing you
Should I fly to Tenerife
Or should I take a coach to Crieff.

Buying brochure books on travel
My summer spot I could unravel
Should I book a tour of Rome
Or should I wallow nearer home.

Might I walk the hills and glens
By climbing higher to the Bens
May I take off to New York
Or spend a week in County Cork.

The choice is really most confusing
Confusion which is quite amusing
Perhaps I need some exercise
Avoiding Customs and Excise.

And then to think about expense
Travellers' cheques, pounds and pence
My pocket sure would know the difference
To visit auntie's place in preference!

Norma A MacArthur

SUMMER HOLIDAYS

The place was in turmoil
The rooms were a mess
The family were excited
The pets distressed
For we were off, away
Two weeks of sun and sand,
Palm trees, blue oceans and coconut milk
Not to mention Disneyland.
The characters were delightful
The park was just great
The attractions fantastic
Except for one date.
The 18th of August loomed dull and dark
For that was the day we would leave that great park,
And return back home to an ordinary place
Where life goes on at a slower pace.

Tamsin Burley

ON A BEACH IN JUNE

On a beach in June,
That's where I'd like to be.
Where the sun always shines,
Just glistening at me,

Where dolphins swim
And birds fly,
Where I can relax
And watch time go by.

A holiday that never ends,
A place to make new friends.

Where horses gallop
And children play,
A place where the sun
Never goes away.

And at night, a full moon would come.
And a sky filled with stars,
I'd keep one safe
Hidden with flowers
Arranged in a vase.

So, on a beach in June,
That's where I'd like to be,
Where the sun always shines,
Just glistening at me.

Kelly Hearne (13)

HOLIDAY BLUES

We waited hours at Gatwick
But still were on the ground
The pilot had gone missing,
Thank goodness he was found.

We reached our destination,
The hotel was half built,
The swimming pool looked tempting
But it was full of silt.

The staff seemed to ignore us
We might as well not speak
Because they knew no English,
We had not mastered Greek.

A lady said she'd help us,
Said we could use her yacht,
With miles of sandy beaches,
The sea, the sun, the lot.

But when at last we saw it
Our hearts sank with a thud.
It was a rotting houseboat
Half buried in the mud.

Our holiday's now over,
So back to work and then
Start saving money. To go
On holiday again.

Jeanne Walker

AT THE WATER HOLE

Lolloping across the plain
A lion with a shaggy mane
The antelope have run away
There is no shade in which to lay

A scorching sun at noon sits high
The ground for miles is hard and dry
Hyenas squabble in the heat
Supplies are short of tender meat

Vultures circle overhead
Each hoping that he'll soon be fed
And at the empty water hole
A rhino stands, a lonely soul

Clouds roll in, but only tease
The withered grass and naked trees
Thin elephants walk slowly by
As Africa is heard to sigh.

Kim Montia

Summer (?) Holiday

Hardly summer in this place,
As the noise of the engine drones on,
And the warm air oozing past my thigh
Belies the temperature of the air outside,
Where ice still thrives on frozen lakes
And snow-clad hills look bleak and bare -
Till the sun shines out from behind a cloud
And transforms the scene before me
      To a sparkle.

And later, as we gaze from balconies
Across a slightly wind-ruffled fjord
To snow-capped mountains
Catching the last rays of dying sun
      So late at night,
Silence reigns, and, holding our breath,
We drink in the life-giving awareness
Of your beauty in nature,
And the gift of Your Presence,
      Which will never cease.
Hardly summer in this place.
      Just the warmth of Your Peace.

Anne Byron

UP HERE WHEN I FLY

Up here when I fly
High above these billowy white clouds
The sky so blue and serene
The sun shining brightly
I drift
Far into a distant world
A place of pleasant dreams
Free from realities and groans
And dreams are almost real
There I remain
Till I hear the touch down message
Bringing me back to realities.
The sights are beautiful
And scenes are breathtaking
Faces looks relaxed and fun seeking
Then I wonder
How long these will last
And I remember the memory bank
Can be a world of pleasant recollections
That comes with whiffs of nostalgia
Bringing temporary contentment.
Till the next holiday comes along
And I go shooting off again
Above the billowy white clouds!

Jennifer Abdulazeez

POETIC DREAM

To fly with you
through space and time
over mountain-top
and river-line
To twist and turn
through misty cloud
Holding hands
all Heaven-bound,
To explore each planet
here and there
Gaze down at people
unaware,
To float through debris
of bygone age
with the trace of famine
and wars and plague
To explore the view
of Heaven's door
on wispy cloud
with many more
Souls like we -
What mystery!
What joy we'd see
Twin-souls we'd be . . .

And God looks down
And smiles!

Mary Skelton

DESTINATIONS

Discarding glossy holiday brochures she sighs,
No desire to tread well worn tourist paths,
Spend days on beach obliterated
By sun seeking hordes in varying shades of tan.

Taking coffee alfresco
She surveys home surroundings.
Bees buzz around honeysuckle,
Sparrows fight for position on nut feeder mesh.
Chaffinch preferring ground level
Feeds on dropped crumbs.
Twittering friends, waiting turn, flutter in
And out of plum tree foliage.
Cat sighted,
Sudden mass exodus occurs;
Garden momentarily silent.
A few doors down puppy dog yaps
Then silence
Broken by solitary bee.

Tilting face to morning sun she smiles.
No packed airports, no foreign customs,
No bustling tourist traps:
Time had come to enjoy nature's
Tranquillity on her own doorstep.

Julia Cutting

SUMMER HOLIDAY

A day of rest from my normal application,
I don't have to drive to my work's location.
I don't have to put on my usual coat,
Or drive past that smelly old moat.

Today I'm free from my work at last,
No more signing contracts, leave that in the past.

This relaxing break is extremely refreshing,
Where am I going? You'll have to keep guessing.
A holiday I've looked forward to all year long,
Is about to begin, I'm off to Hong Kong!

My goodness it's hot, what a powerful sun,
But I've only just got here, it's only just begun.
Hong Kong is a place of wondrous delights,
I like the smells, but I love the sights.

After lots to see and lots to do,
It's finally over, my holiday's through.
Now that it's the end of my vacation,
It's back to work at my usual location.

The thought of putting on my usual coat,
The thought of driving past that smelly old moat,
Makes me feel numb, makes me feel bad,
And makes me feel awful and incredibly sad.
However, my memories of summer will never fade,
Memories are wonderful, whenever they're made.

Kellyann Cochrane (12)

TOMORROW AND TOMORROW AND TOMORROW

But yesterday, or the day before or when?
Away from this dreary, rain-drenched city
To where the sun always shines
And the soft, gentle breeze blows
From the azure sky to the hot, golden sand,
Where at sunset the fishermen slip their moorings
Hopeful of a good night's haul for market.
At dawn one can sit at the harbour entrance
As the sailing fleet returns,
Heading for the old, well-worn walls.
A coach toots its horn to herald an inland tour
Where the air's clear, mountains stark and legends abound
Hidden behind fern and reeds where gurgling rivers play.
A true view of the local people and their land.
No sunbathing for them, just struggle with arid ground,
Praying for rain to fill the mountain streams
And sustain their daily foods.
Totally different from my own world.
A pleasant, rural land where life is slow.
The earth's size has decreased and simple life rare,
Spoilt by the tramp of tourists' feet.
I know that I am blessed and savour
My peaceful seas and skies and countryside.

Tilla B Smith

HOLIDAY MYSTIQUE

The Bay of Tangier is a wonderful sight
Particularly when seen on a starry night,
The sea is black, the stars twinkle white,
Reflecting down, upon the sea's might
There's a traceried pattern of luminous light.

Down in the Casbah the magic goes on
The snake-charmer's melody has just begun,
The cobra itself sways like some pendulum
When it out pops its basket to join in the fun
The beady eyes speaking, its mouth remaining dumb.

Elsewhere in the Casbah there is bustle and commotion
The crowd is at large shows pent-up emotion,
To see all the sights, and evinces every exertion,
To partake in the charms of this exotic location
Which will never be erased in a lifetime's duration.

High on the hill stands the King's mansion
There in this shaded, secluded and sequestered expansion,
Life is more sedate, and with a golden dimension,
Even though, still a game of chance within, glamourous connotation
The proportion is majestic within its feudal convention.

This the high and the mighty, the low and the lowly
Find their own strata of life which to them is the more glowy,
Yet amid this exuberance of might, majesty and notoriety,
That fame and fortune either or does or does not extend to its society
The Tangerian Bay knows its own sobriety.

Renée Duckworth

The Storm Petrel

Mother Carey's chicken purrs and calls,
In the breeding colony, as night falls.
It feeds and paddles on the water by day,
Saint Peter's namesake, or so they say.
The smallest seabird with sooty brown feathers,
Masterful in flight through all kinds of weather.
And to those who believe in more than chance,
A little bird of much significance.
Mater Cara, help us, the sailors would often say,
As they helped her chickens find the food that day.

G E Khandelwal

THE ILLUSTRIOUS SCOT
(AN ODE TO ALEX FERGUSON)

Battle planning wizard, tactician supreme,
A trophy hunter whose hunger for silverware
makes his eyes gleam.

A master motivator of players who have everything,
Instilling hunger and desire to climb higher.
The work ethic is important you don't win titles
with pretty football alone.

To be a winner, that is his driving force,
His *modus operandi* is to try and win every game
and stay the course.

A passionate nature, unshakeable in belief.
Outbursts sometimes regrettable
but in the heat of the moment understandable.

Battle planning wizard Alex Ferguson,
the illustrious Scot.
A trophy hunter whose hunger for silverware
makes him give it all he's got.

Ian Barton

RINGING UP THE CHANGES

We'll meet again - don't know where - don't know when
But we'll meet again - one boxing day.
I lost this time - not in my prime
But I'll belt you next time you come my way.
Gone up a weight - But I still cannot wait
Till the stars above you shine.
That belt will be mine in the ring - this loss don't mean a thing
For I'll finish you off and that will be fine.
Been boxing a long time as you know - and when I land that blow
Those stars will shine for you.
You'll take to your bed - your face will be red
But you'll be feeling blue.
See you next time my friend - then it will be the end
But I doubt that, that you'll see.
You'll be out of this world - when that belt is unfurled
It will be round the waist of me.
Bye, bye for now - we'll meet and how
Happy will be that day.
It will be goodbye - When this little I
Takes you title away.
I'm not one to gloat - but when it comes to the vote
I'm a much better boxer by far.
I may have to scrape - but when I'm in good shape
I'll buy myself a car.
But don't worry mate - it still won't be too late
For you to pick up the pieces again.
Then perhaps we'll meet - and it will be a treat
to see who's the better of we two.
You've had your time - now it is mine
I'll still be looking out for you!

Jon El Wright & Jackdaw

JUST REMEMBER

How strong the love I have for you,
that when I'm gone
will emanate from levelled ground
and reach you.
For when you spare a thought for me,
I'll be there by your side.
When you are sad, my arms
will comfort you.
Should you ever need me, close your eyes
And I will love you.
Just remember!

T G Bloodworth

BOYS

I think boys are a pain in the neck,
And are really annoying,
They are football, football crazy,
And are also zany.
They hit, punch and pinch you,
And they seem to act stupid,
They are wimpy, slimy things,
And scare me because they're so ugly.
When they try to sing or dance,
Their voices turn all squeaky,
But now I'm used to them so much,
Because I've got two brothers at home
And I'd like to say one final sentence,
I hate boys!

Kirsty Towle (9)

BLACK VALLEY

Stories of the black valley,
And its evil spirits that lurk.
A trip to be made alone,
For others scared of getting hurt!
Guess with adrenaline flowing,
Managed to beat any fears.
With locals trying to stop me,
Saying of lost ones through tears!
Jeep loaded with supplies,
Off with the early morning sun.
Along ragged, dusty mountain roads,
Now answers hopefully won.
Then a small mountain village,
But no one spoke my tongue.
A woman crushing grapes,
Wanted me to join in her fun!

Their expressions told me something,
But knew I had to press on.
With roads crumbling beneath me,
The mountain saying I didn't belong!
Determination kept me going,
Stomach churned at the drop.
For one step wrong I knew,
I would have had my lot!
Driving now at an angle,
Fear hit me, as I slid on a rock.
Then there was the black valley,
Fire eaten, why life had stopped!
Remains of chard settlements,
Proving once life was rich.
From up here it just looks,
Like the ground's been painted with pitch!

Walking in the depths of the valley,
Black rocks cascade from the sky.
A daunting feeling of devastation,
But it didn't smell, wonder why?
Dumbstruck by this black mass,
Had to rest and quench my thirst.
Staring aimlessly at the ground,
Thought I detected a shoot had burst!
Then as I looked more closely,
It was as if the earth was coming alive.
Excitement flowed within me,
For the valley was going to thrive!
As I returned to my jeep,
The only spirits, mine lifted on high.
Knowing I could return with good news,
For the black valley, it was goodbye!

Ann Beard

AUSTRIA

Austria
Where the great blue Danube always flows.

Austria
Where the mountains are snow-capped and the
ice caves are cold.

Austria
Where views are unbelievable and
lakes are warm and calm.

Austria
Where you can have lunch next to the river in Vienna.

Austria
Where you can stay up all night in cafes.

Austria
Where you can listen to folk songs all day long.

Ben Forbes (12)

AFRICA

Africa is the place to go,
To see the cheetahs run so fast;
It's a big, big place so,
Africa is the place to go.

Africa is the place to go,
To see the lions' killings,
The leopards hunting so;
Africa is the place to go.

Africa is the place to go,
To see the blazing sun,
It's lots of fun so;
Africa is the place to go.

Africa is the place to go,
To see the monkeys stealing,
The witch doctors healing so;
Africa is the place to go.

Africa is the place to go,
Where the hyenas laugh,
And the giraffes are ever so tall,
So Africa is the place to go!

Alexander Foot (12)

CANADA

Canada
Where the crisp snow
crunches under your feet.

Canada
Where brown bears roam
and sparkling fish leap.

Canada
Where the hairy caribou
run wild and free.

Canada
Where the Inuit hunt
for seal and blubber.

Canada
Where the animals
own the land.

Canada
Where the CN Tower is
higher than the skyline.

Canada
Where people speak two languages
French and English.

Canada
Where the Rockies are
the greatest mountains on Earth.

Canada
Where the prairies
grow so much wheat.

Canada
Where the Northern Lights
brighten up the sky.

Adam Carter (12)

NEW YORK

New York, New York,
Famous for its Statue of Liberty,
Tall, noble and inspiring.
The helicopter trip around it is spectacular.

New York, New York,
Famous for its Empire State Building,
Once the tallest building in the world:
From the top you can see the best of New York.

New York, New York,
Famous for its Central Park.
The shaded banks to picnic on
And the TV set for 'Friends'.

New York, New York,
Famous for Fifth Avenue,
Some of the greatest shops in the world,
Tiffany's and Elizabeth Arden.

New York, New York,
Home of the Natural History Museum,
Mummies and cave men
And always exciting exhibitions.

New York, New York
Famous for everything:
Why don't you go there yourself and see?

Kayleigh Bromell (12)

TO DARREN
(Our Tour Guide in Toronto)

Now have you met our Darren?
A very friendly chap
He is a 'mine' of information
I guess he deserves a clap.
He is our Tour Manager
Or so his badge portrays
And he is so full of knowledge
Sometimes I'm in a daze!
He hops upon the bus
As gay as any lark
Well - except this morning -
Was he jogging round the park?
But I am sure we all forgive him
And wish him luck with future 'Tours'
Altogether tourists -
Hands together for applause.

Esther Hawkins

Lytham

Steeped in the nostalgia of bygone generations,
Trapped in time unable to capture times past,
Reluctantly moving into the twentieth century
As the century closes to give birth to the twenty first!
Seas which once lapped golden sands
Now keep well distant from the shore.
Insidiously creeping across the mudflats,
Bringing with it reminders of foregone times.
The paddling pool, old and cracked,
Sandpit overgrown with grass
Stand empty beneath the old sea wall.
When once they would be the centre of activity
Ringing with the laughter of innocents
Expanses now empty save for the forlorn calling of the gulls.
Abandoned boats stranded on flats of mud.
Seen through the misted visions of memories.
Of the loving eyes of its ageing population.

Teresa Booth

MY HOLIDAY

It's time to take a holiday; I definitely need a break,
Thank God he's opened the door, I've booked now and
Got a cheap rate. Guess where I'm going . . .
I'm off to the sun, hello Barbados here I come.
The beautiful sand and glorious sun, and the lovely fruits
It's just like paradise; you should have come;
I thank God for his handiwork; he's the artist of our world
We must thank him and praise him, he is amazing.

Sandra Rose

SUMMER HOLIDAYS

You asked in not more than thirty lines or less,
I will try and do just that will do my very best.
As I sit in my room, called my den, it comes back
Thinking of our holidays gone by that's a fact
No travelling around the world no blooming fear not us
We the wife and myself when our children (no fuss)
Were growing up was to take them the three of them
Tony the eldest then our daughter Pat plus the youngest
Our son John was to go to Ramsgate on Sea did depend
On a neighbour of ours Jim and wife Dolly a friend
Or should I have said friends we say God bless
They are not with us any more both in God's hands you see
My old mind goes back to the good times we the five to be
Exact our children were born during World War Two
Myself serving our country in the army that's true
So of course it had to be a few years after yes by golly
We stayed with a relation of our Jim and yes his Dolly
Bed and breakfast was the order of the day good that
A Mrs Plummer was the relation that took the five of us in
Travelling down to Ramsgate on my Robin three wheeler sing
Guess what we used to sing to a seaside resort
Ten Green Bottles Hanging On The Wall no more to report
After all only thirty lines my memories would fill a
Book I will count up the lines up till now I say
Twenty two just eight to jolly well go lets see
How great those summer holidays were to us to be
Not much money about in those days of old but then
We still enjoyed going to the seaside we did depend
On the money earned at my place of work understand
My wife May myself Just Tom think the holidays grand

Just Tom Sexton

Shhhh...

Shh shh, lap lap
Shh shh, lap lap lap

No-one around
with only sound
of the swishing sea
as you sit silently
Clear blue skies
weren't you wise
to take this time
some lemon and lime
and holiday trip for two.

Shh shh, lap lap
Shh shh, lap lap lap
Now curl your toes
and wrinkle your nose
take in the sight
as you curl up tight
or stretch out long
and hear summer's song
say, 'No matter what
you know you've got
a holiday dream come true.'

Angel Robinson

IN MY MIND'S EYE
(I dedicate this poem to Jenny Stone)

A dream of far off places
Places where we are free,
Free from the constraints of life
A life that so entraps me.

A dream of sunkissed beaches
Beaches of glistening white sands
Sands who's shores are caressed
By a vast, blue, oceanic hand.

A dream of Technicolor sunsets
Sunsets reflected on crystal clear sea,
Sea that stretches beyond the minds eye
Beyond life, beyond you and me.

A dream we all dream of escaping
Escaping to our own paradise,
A paradise made of all our dreams
Dreams where you don't pay a price.

Can you picture this dream
A paradise lost completely in time,
A time that can be now and forever
Because forever it's locked inside your mind.

This dream is your dream holiday
Where you go everywhere but don't take a step,
The steps are only travelled in your mind
Because in your mind this secret place is kept . . .

Jo Howson

BRIGHTON BY THE SEA

No foreign holidays for the family
We're off to Brighton by the Sea
We've packed and loaded up the car
Ready for the journey which isn't far
So no need for a ferry or a plane
Just a car and a map to keep us sane

Forget the office, forget the boss
Enjoy bumper cars and candyfloss
Peer through prestigious windowpanes
Buy antiques and jewellery from 'The Lanes'
We could shop for weeks
In this shoppers' paradise set in cobbled streets

Brighton, premier seaside resort, no less
It's better than anywhere else, it's simply the best
It's got fish and chips and tomato sauce
Wrapped in the local paper of course
It's got the West Pier and the Palace Pier
Fairs, carnivals, culture, it's all here

The shingle's left behind as the tide goes out
The jelly shoes too as the kids run about
Splashing at the water's edge, running across golden sands
Sporting suntans and wearing bright armbands
This could be the 'Med', not Brighton by the Sea
It's great to be here, it's great to enjoy the variety

The sun's gone down, it's the end of the day
But not the end of the fun, no way
Let's enjoy the nightlife, the twinkling lights
The promenade, the pier and all the other sights
A romantic dinner overlooking the sea
And home to our cosy B & B

Alexandra Ayton

UNNECESSARY

I don't need to travel,
I've no need to roam,
My own summer holiday
Is here, at my home.

> Sitting in sunshine for hours and hours,
> Weeding the garden, planting more flowers;
> Feeding the birds and watching them squabble
> Over small crumbs of bread, the nuts and the sorrel.

If the sky turns grey
Or the winds blow cold,
I've shelves of books
With stories of old.

> I've letters to write, and paintings to do,
> Listening to music, with needlework too.

My house is so small that it's never a bore
To finish the cleaning and household chores.
I can go to the club with neighbours of mine
And have a good chat over glasses of wine.

I never feel lonely, although I'm alone;
Retirement is bliss! I thank God for my home.
> So I've no need to travel
> Nor even to roam,
> My life's one long holiday
> Here, at home.

Elsa D Wilson

THE BIG APPLE

The sea of yellow cabs
Stretch as far as the eye can see
If you want to travel anywhere
Just shout 'Taxi!'

Twisting, turning through the crowds
People rushing from place to place
Some people carry bags of food or clothes
Others carry a briefcase

Buildings seems so close together
The skyscrapers seem so high
You look up in amazement
They seem to even touch the sky

Everyone here seems so hyper
Sometimes not even having time to eat
Now I know why this place is known as
The city that never sleeps

You can visit many places in the city
Including Central Park
Though like many places in New York
It's not safe to visit after dark

There are so many places to go
And so many things to do
If you enjoy an exciting atmosphere
This is the place for you

The Statue of Liberty stands high
Looking over the city
Which, twenty-four hours a day
Is always so busy.

M Saqib Hussain

SUMMER HOLIDAY

It was and is the holiday
I will never forget
I enjoyed so much
I felt so relaxed
so cool
so entertained
in the calm and tranquillity
of Eastbourne
and its seaside
so beautiful
so clean . . . so calm
I felt I have become
part of it
I still feel
if I do not die
and I have the resources
then I should reside there
to become part of it
in every moment . . . every day's
kaleidoscopic life's livings
to understand, appreciate and admire
this affinity of Eastbourne and myself.

Ghazanfer Eqbal

LOOKING FORWARD

Sun, sea and even sand,
our holiday has already been planned.
Nice hot weather, plenty of ice-cream,
all of the things that we often dream.
Clubs for the night-time, fair for the day,
the kind of place you would love to stay.
Got to pack, it's time to go,
back home where we only have rain or snow.

Catherine Whittaker

THIS SUMMER

This place continues to boil with unrest,
And yet, in these burnt times of the summer,
The sun still winks at me through the leaves.
I drive, but I want to fly away,
To another day,
Another season,
Where they look after
What's given
For a reason,
And don't just scorn where they're living.
This is just too much today;
I need another strong sugared coffee!

Naomi Elisa Price

HOLIDAYS

Holidays, my holidays, not one but many
Engrained forever in my heart
From the elegance of Paris, the history of Rome
The magic of Venice, the cathedral of Cologne
Delays at the airport, gales on the sea
Overnight stops, the awful tea
Mozart in Salzburg, Beethoven in Bonn
Opera in Verona, Vienna's song
Lake Garda's beauty, Jerusalem's fame
Fjords in Norway, flamenco in Spain
Sorrento and Amalfi, Pompeii and Capri
Wonderful places I was lucky to see
Caravans in Scotland, apartments by the sea
Children's joyous laughter, happy and free
So much excitement, so much pleasure
So many memories to keep and to treasure
But when each holiday was over
And my journey was done
I wasn't sad, I didn't moan
But felt my heart uplifted
By the joy of coming home

Barbara E Stubbs

HOLIDAY MOODS

Throughout the days
With thoughts of you
My summer holidays
And skies of blue
The calming seas
With colours of azure
These are my dreams
Who would ask for more

Brenda Holland

SUMMER HOLIDAYS - THEN AND NOW

I don't think the holidays we used to have
Would satisfy kids of today:
Our pleasures were simple - just buckets and spades,
Picnicking, paddling and play.
We enjoyed every minute, it didn't cost much,
We stayed in a nice 'B and B';
If the weather was poor, we had fun on the pier;
There were always new wonders to see!

Today it's a different kettle of fish:
The 'norm' is a flight on a plane:
Quite blasé, the children jet off on their hols
To Florida, Turkey or Spain.
I just wonder if it's not rather a shame,
They've done it all when they're so young:
Waiting in patience for when one's grown up,
In my book, is part of the fun.

Corinne Lovell

SUMMER HOLIDAY

For years I saved to go on a cruise abroad,
I talked it over, with my good Lord.
A bit apprehensive of going on my own,
But Jesus saw to it, I was not alone.
Unfortunately we had very rough seas,
Every one was sick, down on their knees.
Two and a half days of sun, that was all,
The rest of the days were all rock and roll.
As the ship rolled to and fro,
Our food on the table did not know which way to go.
The swimming pool was sloshing about,
So they had to let all the water out.
Two passengers died, all very sad,
Another got a fish bone stuck in his throat; that was bad.
A helicopter came and took him to land,
But other than that, I found the trip grand.

Sylvia M Harbert

THE WAY THEY WERE

School was out, and without a doubt.
What stretched ahead,
Day after day after day.
Was the summer holiday.
Thoughts that only lead,
To play and play and play.

Unheard of Majorca, Ibiza and the like,
Unheard of travel on boat, train and plane.
Enough to ride your bike,
Country lanes to hike.
To fill the days, ten thousand ways.
Picnics in the wood,
Paddling by the brook,
Helping with the hay.
How bright the sun, how great the fun.
Happy days, country ways.

Stress, a word uninvented then,
No TV to keep us in.
Children's Hour with Uncle Mac,
Dick Barton Special Agent only he,
Could keep us back after tea.
With luck a Saturday matinee.
Roy Rogers, Will, Gene Autrey.
A longer trip to river or sea,
Would be planned to a tee.
Rides on a donkey,
Boats to row, happy and free.
Cockles and mussels, from a flask of tea.
Simple pleasures for a simpler time.
Would it were still mine.

Rose Marie Morris

ARCADIA BALTIC CRUISE

Across the Northern Sea
From England's little isle
To see the Baltic countries
We cruised for many a mile

Sped onto Norway's Oslo
The Vikings Museum to see
Visiting Viegland's sculpture park
To forget our modesty!

To Denmark's city Copenhagen
The Tivoli Gardens toured
Taxi back to our ship
Was really where we scored!

To Stockholm's Stadhaus touring
In grandness we must see
All back to our ship
That's after a shopping spree

Across we cruised to stop
At Helsinki, find land's port
It's such a lovely country
Much bigger than I thought

Next we visit Leningrad
See treasures of the past
All displayed for the tourist
Whose rubies vanish fast

Fifteen days of luxury
We tasted every day
Back home to dear England
Is where I want to stay.

Alice M Archer

NEVER ALONE

Setting out on holiday
Leaving cares behind
Heading for a new land
I wonder what I'll find
Trees that sway like dancers
Sand glistening like gems
Even though I'm on my own
I'll be making many friends.

Basking in the sunshine
That blazes in the sky
Birds of many colours
Wondrous, flying by
Here on my desert Island
Fishing, with my rod
Creatures are my new friends
Alone here, but with God.

G Read

PERFECT BLISS

I am on my summer holiday
My home is a million miles away

I am standing on the shore of the sea
Watching dolphins swim past me

I am walking barefoot along the sand
With my summer romance holding my hand

I am lying on the beach watching birds fly high
Watching them twist and turn in the sky

I am licking a cool ice-cream
And going on theme park rides which make me scream

I am walking with a gentle breeze
It's blowing pollen from the fields, that's making me sneeze

I am learning to do the national dance
Watch me turn, watch me prance

I wish you could see me, I wish you could see this
It's total, complete and utter perfect bliss

Amy Webb

Mud Eater

Vivid impressions remain, a vision of utter loveliness,
A hauntingly beautiful, wild and rugged terrain, bathed
in liquid gold, awesome to behold.
A landscape of unimaginable contrasts, of
incomparable charm, designed to disarm the
cynic and the worldly wise, sun drenched
cliff tops, blue/green waters, cloudless skies.

Lavender scented plateaus, deep ravines and gullies,
springs, spas and fountains, snow capped mountain peaks,
chaotic Verdun gorges, shrouded in mystique, what
secrets might they betray, could they but speak,
witnessed through the ages, a seismic
upheaval of these proportions does not happen in a day.
Their history would fill a million pages.

And the legendary wind, 'mud eater of the Rhone',
like a giant carpet beater, every tree, stick, leaf
and stone a target for its purifying breath,
cleansing the ozone, and in its aftermath.
a sky scrubbed crystal blue,
every blade of grass, tree and flower
a brighter hue, palm trees sway, their branches dancing
to its forceful tune.

Mighty 'mistral' the wind that bears the poets
illustratious name, to the glorious Côte d'Azure from
whence he came, I'm loath to say goodbye
So 'Au revoir' I shall return for sure,
your scenic wonders further to explore,
unforgettable haute Provence, I'll be back - first chance.

Mary G Kane

SOMEWHERE IN ANDALUCIA

Come with me,
Let's discover the mystery
Of a magical place,
Touched by God's grace.

Where its Mediterranean balcony
Gazes languorously out to sea.
Pretty senoritas promenade with pride,
Chaperoning grandmothers at their side.

This whitewashed pueblo of the Spanish Riviera
Nestles on the edge of a pine clad sierra.
Narrow streets, enchanting squares,
Romantic churches to offer prayers.

Just along a country road
Lies a place I wish were my abode.
An isolated hacienda
Regales in rustic, rural splendour.

The alarm clock shatters my holiday dreams,
Gone forever or so it seems.
But maybe I'll return quite soon
To my Andalucian Brigadoon.

Ian Fyles

IN THE ARMS OF THE MOON

Wasted weak moon between curtains
That rocks in dream's pendulum high
Lacking the power to steal my midnight mood
Pursuing starry spheres of melancholy symmetry
Wearily brooding imprint in the shadowy grey
Closing the flowery petals scented stock
Pacing the seconds 'til we meet again
In dusty dark-eyed street lamp gloom
Trembling kisses cling light tongued
Despite the long passage of thought
When roughly together beneath the weak moon
Shame had no words to our love
We two thinning the night between moonshine
Vanished the blanks and the regrets in our lives
Curving the scattered stars to their night quarters
Pale moons presence shines and grins in the frost

Christine Denise Wells

Maiden Voyage

Scared breathless enter sardine can
Extinguish appeasing cigarette airline ban
Maiden flight madam unbelievably scared
Welded to sit never utters one word
Plane touches down, passengers disembark
Camouflage fears aboard, coach ghostly dark
Unpack apparel, washed, brushed and dusted
Womanly wild imaginings, unleashed so lusted
Spanish sun bathe sickly white skin
Four vestal virgins searching for sin
Wild heady nights, dance flirt and shriek
Stalking the early hours hotel creep
Yellow sandy beach beckons body unclad
Fears relinquished, warm sun makes me glad
Warm calm sea enjoying swimming each day
Fears about flying light years away
Missed many travels through fears, but then
Fears over come madam, shall fly again

Ann Hathaway

SUMMER HOLIDAY

Summer holidays, summer holidays,
we're lying on the beach,
getting a nice brown tan,
then we go splashing into the sea,
to cool ourselves down.

Summer holidays, summer holidays,
we have a lovely picnic on the sand,
then we build sandcastles,
and oh what fun we have.

Summer holidays, summer holidays,
now the fun, lovely holiday has ended,
everyone is sad,
as they all count the days till the next fun one.

Jenny Youngs

SUMMER HOLIDAYS

Summer holidays are here at last,
it's time to take a break,
to sit back, relax and enjoy the time ahead.

Donkey rides along the beach,
hot sun, sea and sand;
ice-creams on the pier and children having fun!

Days out with the family exploring
in the deserted woods.
Cycling through the country on narrow, windy roads.

Swimming at the pool followed by picnics
in the crowded, public park;
then spending lots of money shopping till it's dark!

Rebecca Heard (14)

THE BEACH

I'm visited in the autumn,
People walking dogs,
They come,
Then they go.

I'm deserted in the winter,
The rain and snow,
They come,
Then they go.

I'm occupied in the spring,
Visitors and guests,
They come,
Then they go.

I'm packed in the summer,
When the sun shines down so brightly,
And birds come out nightly,
Children come and play,
And tourists stay all day,
The children will say,
They're having their best day,
And they haven't shed a tear,
'Cause it's their favourite time of year.

Sophie Walter (13)

SUMMER

These things remind me of summer:
Running, shot,
Water, sand,
Ice-cream, spades,
Beach balls, waves.

Krazy golf, sun,
Buzzing bees, fun:
Flowers, swings,
Surfboard dings.

Bananas, cream,
Toys, streams.
Rounders, games,
Dancing, fame.
These things remind me of summer.

Karla Webb (14)

Australia

Australia,
A place of sun,
Full of beaches, bathers and heat.

Australia,
A place of growth,
Full of new and stylish buildings.

Australia,
A place of fun,
Going to work or busy shopping.

Australia,
A place of kangaroos,
Bouncing and jumping everywhere.

Australia,
A place of fruit,
With a kiwi on every tree.

Australia,
A place of dreams,
The place you want to go to.

Australia.

Ashley Withey (12)

AFRICA

Africa,
Where the trees grow tall
And jungles are deep.
Where the hyenas laugh
And the monkeys swing.
Where the lions roam free
And the cheetahs run fast.
Where the elephants stomp
And beautiful birds sing.
Where the Sahara burns hot
And the Savannah grows green.
In a blazing hot sun,
You lick cool ice-creams.
With golden sandy beaches
And sparkling silver seas.
Africa is surely . . .
A place of dreams.

Muna Ngenda

ITALIA

Italia
Where nice hot sun
Beams down your neck.

Italia
The Tower of Pisa, the Coliseum of Rome
A plate of historic architecture.

Italia
The food is terrific - spaghetti and pizza
Completely delicious.

Italia
Every shop is up-to-date
And all the clothes are chic.

Italia
You'll never get bored
The night life is jumping.

Italia
During the day you can see
A football match, yes, there are plenty of those!

Italia
Home of Ferrari, Bugati and Fiat
A place of brilliant cars.

Italia
Turin, Milan and Naples
A place of wonderful cities.

Italia!

Ryan Kewley (12)

AUSTRALIA

Australia
The best for surf
Shining sun, magic sea.

Australia
The best for animals
Koala, kiwi, bird and kangaroo.

Australia
The best for sights
Ayres Rock, the Sydney Opera House.

Australia
The best for food
Kiwi fruit and BBQ fish.

Australia
The best for people
Friendly, calm and trustful.

Australia
The best for me
Lots and lots of fun.

Sarah Heard (11)

FLORIDA SUN

F laming overhead, it can burn you if you're not careful,
L ovely to tan in though beside the pool.
O n the beach scorching your feet,
R ays of the sun beating down on you.
I n the pool it heats the water for you,
D azing your eyes in the boiling sun.
A ll the time, sun all day!

I n the city the sun is at its best,
S un never dies except for the night.

S un is great, boiling and scorching,
U p in the sky closer to the heat of the sun.
N ever ending sun all the time!
N ever to stay inside away from the sun.
Y ears and years of excellent sun!

Katie Furniss (12)

EASTBOURNE

Eastbourne is great! Eastbourne is so very good!
Nudge, nudge, wink, wink, is that quite understood?
No, now be serious - sit up and pay attention!
Everybody is so merry here, straying away from stiff, starchy convention.

Jack and Jane are busy - so busy eating ice-cream and building sandcastles with great uncertainty -
Bemused Jacob, the architect smiles at them wearily as he steals glances at them while eating his hot pasty -
Belinda rather fancies the dark haired boy who in turn feels the same way but is too shy to make a pass at her
And she studies his profile from her mirror while teasing her hair into a strange coiffure.

Everybody is invited to run in the egg and spoon race
Even grandad comes along not wishing to lose face;
The sun is our friend today as it beams and transforms the darkest holes into sunshined pits
And Jacob leaves his deckchair to jig, jitterbug and boogie to the radio's blast of the latest popular hits.

Jane is having a mini battle eating candyfloss in the strong breeze
Grandad licks his lips as he prepares to eat saveloys and gives the tomato paste tube a mighty squeeze
And I am knee deep in the sea with my bucket looking for seashells to take back home with me -
It is so good, so relaxed and happy - I really wish you were here to see.

It's seven o'clock and we prepare to leave taking ourselves and our
    wares with us
On arrival at the hotel it is a garden of flowers - they just can't do
    enough for us
The sumptuous meal is, wait for it, pumpkin pie, lobster, crab, potatoes
    and lots of greens
And the proprietor has offered to escort us to more fun spots of
    Eastbourne - to feast our eyes on the lovely scene.

Margaret Andrews

MOVE OVER - NOAH

If I went to the desert it would rain - guaranteed,
When pitching a tent - it's wellies I need.
The view from a coach is one - just of mist -
They're only illusions - those beaches sun-kissed!
I could jump on a jet - and see ice on the wing,
I'll stroll down the prom, then feel the wind's sting.
I've the fare for a ferry - look, *dark* clouds overhead,
I must change my route - *watch* 'Travel' instead.
This is the life! But, then, true to form -
The 'heavens' descend, I view the storm.

Beryl Mapperley

The Spanish Senorita

The Spanish senorita and her children walk the sand
Carrying her wares to sell
Held tightly in her hand
One child cries and tells the tale
How much for you senor?
The other one runs ahead
Like walking door to door
The mother clasps a little cup
And begs for pesos sad
When she receives her eyes light up
For now she's feeling glad

The other little ninos
Are running wild today
Trying to help their mother
Walking along the way
Muchas grassias senor they say
How are you today?
Two for a dollar
Usually they say
Or one is free today
Picking bottles out of the sand
For returns at no delay
The tiny Mexican children cry
Almost free today

Glenys M Bowell

AT HOME IN HOLIDAYLAND

Every day is like a holiday,
When you live in the Scottish Highlands.
Every day is like a holiday,
On the mainland or the islands.
What can Spain offer, Italy or Greece,
When you have the Highlands, as beautiful as these?
Life's like a holiday in the Scottish Highlands.

In May, the land is covered in gold,
The rape fields are in full bloom.
And on the hills, and along the roads,
Flowering gorse and broom.

Long summer days and short summer nights,
Sunsets, a sight to behold.
You sing and dance at a Ceilidh-night,
Just as in days of old.

In autumn, the hills are mauve and pink,
The heather is out again.
In woodlands, the mushrooms raise their heads,
Specially after rain.

Watch salmon leap over waterfalls,
See deer in forests up high.
Welcome the first covering of snow,
Skiers searching the sky.

You keep all your airports and motorways,
Crowded beaches, and a noisy hotel,
Where you fight for a place in the swimming pool,
Then talk about the 'holiday from hell'.

Come, see for yourself, and believe when I say:
Scottish Highlands - a heavenly holiday.

Helga I Dharmpaul

LAC ST. BONNET, TRONCAIS

Cool calm lake
surrounded by green oaks
whose massive trunks shelter
this pearl shimmering
under a summer sky.

Fresh clear water
where brown fish glide lazily
over smooth grey stones
occasionally splashing the surface
causing concentric ripples which
circle softly towards the shore.

Six orange pedalos
lie idle by the jetty
reflecting gaily in
the blue-sky waters
like marigolds giving pleasure
in a summer garden.

Graceful as a swan
a white yacht
sails serenely across
briefly furrowing the surface
as it passes
leaving peace undisturbed
in this other Eden.

Kathy Butler

HOLIDAY HELL

Cancel the papers - cancel the milk
Buy a new dress and a scarf made of silk.
Get the suntan - buy a swim hat
Pack the aspirins - must book in the cat.
Call at the doctors, a prescription is due
Sickness tablets, blood pressure pills too.
Turn up that new dress, buy the kids new sandals
Sort out the cases - oh no! Broke at the handles.
I'm off to the bank, what do you mean it's closed
Who's that at the door? Tell them I'm indisposed.
Ironing piled high, washing galore
No time to watch tele, it's just chore after chore.
No you're not going topless, daughters beware
Holiday romances they lead to despair.

Seems to me some of the joy it kills
All this performance - not to mention the bills.
Just to get away into the sun
Three weeks work - to enjoy just one.
I can't relax, I need to sleep . . .
Holidays - I can do without
It's my sanity . . .
I need to keep.

M Ekins

FISTRAL BAY

Grey white tufts hang from the sky,
sun hinting its life to touch the dark waters,
the air ripped by cries of circling gulls.
Great wind driven waves smash upon the rocks,
a million broken drops
hurled towards the sky.

Against the cliff
broken sea climbs ever higher
reaching up and up and up
as though to touch the hand of its Creator,
and offer thanks for the gifts
of life and power.

Full width of bay,
line upon foaming line
crash upon the shore
the sound ceaseless
as the movement.
Awesome power is there,
the power of nature,
of creation;
and its beauty.

The eye can never tire
of watching nature
crafting the forms and shapes
that change without ceasing
until the end of time.

Roy Hedgcock

Seaside Holiday!

Walk along a sandy beach
Where sun-kissed wavelets lap the shore
Feel the tangy, salted air
Upon your face, so fresh and pure.
See the shells beneath your feet
Left there by the ebbing tide
Thrown up by a turbulent sea
And scattered freely far and wide.
Look towards the far horizon
Where King Neptune's holding sway
Controlling thunderous rolling breakers
White-crested waves, heading for the bay.
Faster now the tide is flowing
Coming in towards the shore
Louder now, the sea is calling
Soon you'll hear its mighty roar.
Now, the hungry gulls are flying
Whirling, and screeching their own shrill song
Diving and searching for helpless fishes
Which they hope the sea has brought along.
Satisfied, their hunger abated
They leave the sea for safety inland
But the tide is turning once again
And only ripples in the sand
Show where the sea had covered all
Footprints, seashells, where you stroll
But now, the sea is calm again
King Neptune's back in his own domain
No longer we hear that thunderous roar
It's safe to resume our stroll along the shore.

Margaret McHugh

GO TO CROATIA

G o to Croatia where the sea is blue
O n the town there is lots to do

T o the hotel, it is really nice
O h boy, do they have excellent rice

C roatia is a wonderful place
R un through the sea and splash your face
O n the beach you can sunbathe all day
A nd there's no wind to blow you away
T o the shops I go every day
I n them you don't have much to pay
A nd that's why I think Croatia is so great
    so go there, it's not too late.

Kristina Kastelan

SUBMISSIONS INVITED
SOMETHING FOR EVERYONE

POETRY NOW '99 - Any subject, any style, any time.

WOMENSWORDS '99 - Strictly women, have your say the female way!

STRONGWORDS '99 - Warning! Age restriction, must be between 16-24, opinionated and have strong views. (Not for the faint-hearted)

All poems no longer than 30 lines.
Always welcome! No fee!
Cash Prizes to be won!

Mark your envelope (eg *Poetry Now)* **'99**
Send to:
Forward Press Ltd
Remus House, Coltsfoot Drive,
Woodston,
Peterborough, PE2 9JX

**OVER £10,000 POETRY PRIZES
TO BE WON!**

Judging will take place in October 1999